Glenn Martin is the author of around thirty books. He is an independent scholar and writer. He has written books on ethics and values, the "bigger picture", family history, reflections on experience, and several volumes of poetry. His career includes teaching in high schools, tertiary institutions and adult education programs. He has managed organisations in the community sector, written commentary on employment law, management, ethics and training for professional publications, edited a national magazine for trainers, and designed online education courses.

Glenn lives in Sydney.

Books on ethics and values
by Glenn Martin

Human Values and Ethics in the Workplace (2010)
The Little Book of Ethics: A Human Values Approach (2011)
The Concise Book of Ethics (2012)
A Foundation for Living Ethically (2020)

Books on the bigger picture

Future: The Spiritual Story of Humanity (2020)
A Singular Book of Great Esteem: Life with the I Ching (2025)

A foundation for ethics

Glenn Martin

G.P. Martin Publishing

Published 2026 by G.P. Martin Publishing
Website: www.glennmartin.com.au
Contact: info@glennmartin.com.au

Book layout and cover design by the author.
Printed by Lulu.com
ISBN: 978 1 7644114 1 7 (pbk.)

A catalogue record for this book is available from the National Library of Australia

What are we to say about ethics? It is widely thought to be a contentious field. Is it?

An exalted perspective on ethics

Alfred Huang (2004) says: "If one's attitude is not sincere and whole-hearted, one is not able to distinguish right and wrong."

Lao Tzu (~500 BC) refers to the "superior person". We are suspicious of the word 'superior'. We think it promotes unjustified hierarchies. But think of the superior person as an accomplished person, one who has developed their capacities. Among their accomplishments is virtue.

Richard Rudd (2015), explaining Lao Tzu, says that the person of virtue is one who has surrendered to the natural way, who lives in accord with the universe. A person of virtue displays the unimpeded expression of natural power. This is a person who works (and lives) for the final flowering of human possibility. It is not adherence to a set of conventional rules. It is a guiding purity that pulls us into the future.

Seen in this way, virtue works to heal what is broken in the world. It is not the private possession of superiority. Virtue is the intent of the universe expressed through a human being. When we see it in a person, even flashes of it, we see the certainty of a perfected future for humanity. We remember it, deep within our being.

However, we have to deal with pressing questions about how ethics can operate in our world.

The pressing question about ethics

Will "doing good" be effective in the long run, or does the world require us to be tough, and "do what needs to be done", regardless of ethics? Do the means justify the ends? Can we afford to be ethical? If we are not prepared to "play rough sometimes", will we ever be successful, or even survive?

We know there are many people who feel this way. It has even been turned into a philosophy (I would say, a pseudo-philosophy). In 1960, Milton Friedman claimed that "The only responsibility of business is to maximise profits for shareholders." It has been used as a self-justification ever since, despite its anti-social, immoral thrust. You would have heard people say: "Business is business."

Peter Drucker, who is one of the founders of the discipline of management, offered an alternative proposition in the 1950s: "The purpose of a business is to be found in society. Businesses create customers. And the purpose of profit is to validate the success of the business."

In the first view, ethics is subservient to the self-serving desires of businesspeople. In Drucker's formulation, human society comes first, and business and economics is a subset of that. It must be this way if humanity is to survive. It must be this way for humanity's well-being. See Figure 1.

Next, we should recognise that there can be different conversations about ethics.

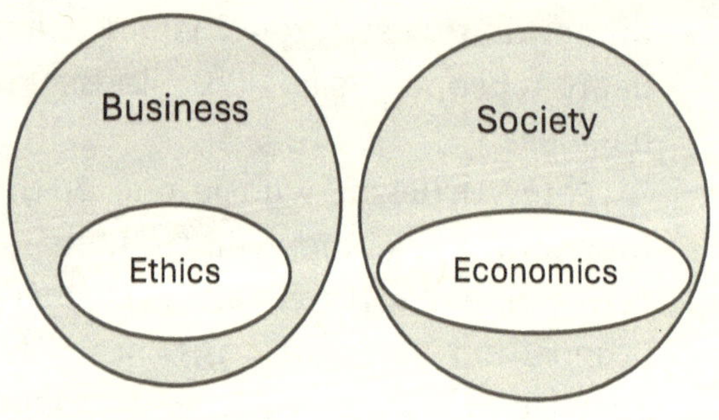

Figure 1

Is ethics about rules for oneself, or rules for everyone?

Let's say there are two conversations about ethics. Not recognising this can lead to confusion in discussions of ethics.

The first conversation is about social groups, and society. What rules should apply to all? How can the rules be enforced? And how can appropriate conduct be fostered, supported and encouraged?

In traditional moral philosophy, the social perspective is articulated through the principle, "Act so as to create the greatest good for the greatest number". This seems sensible, and it is called utilitarianism.

However, it does raise problems. In working to achieve the greatest good for the greatest number, evils may be done to individuals. An example is where a family loses its home because a freeway needs to be built. Many people will benefit from the freeway. Of course, the family is paid "just compensation" for the house, but as we saw in the movie, "The Castle", that does not compensate for the loss of one's home.

The second conversation about ethics is personal. It is about individual responsibility. The philosopher Immanuel Kant argued for this. He said, "Act only according to that maxim by which you can at the same time will that it should become a universal law." In other words, what is right is what you would be willing for everyone else to do as well. This led to an acceptance of duties, and it is called deontology.

There is power in what Kant said, but it conflicts with the first view. Can they be reconciled? Not really. Most philosophers still line up behind one view or the other. The discussion seems to be aimed at simplicity: there is one rule; it's just a question of which one it is.

Rules for everyone	Rules for oneself
Agreement	Personal commitment
Enforcement	Self-discipline
Encouragement	Self-development

Figure 2

This discussion does not resolve whether we should be talking about rules (or principles) for all of society, or rules for the individual (see Figure 2). As we have seen, we could end up talking about two different things.

Virtue ethics

However, there is a third school in moral philosophy: Virtue Ethics. Mostly its advocates refer back to the ancient Greek philosophers, but some modern philosophers have made new observations. Elizabeth Anscombe (in 1958) argued that all the emphasis has been on rules for decision-making. She contended that attention should return to ethics as virtue: What kind of person should we be? What kind of life should we live?

Does this approach make a good substitute for the two rule-based approaches? If we take a rules-based approach, it still leaves virtue as the final question: if I take a particular course of action, what kind of person does it make me? But should we then ignore the two rules? Some philosophers have argued that virtue ethics does not give us a solid-enough footing. It's nice but it's a bit vague. We need some clear rules as a foundation for ethics.

Bear in mind that we also have to account for social norms changing over time. Australia had a convict past, and now we think the whole idea of convicts is wrong. And the treatment of convicts was generally brutal. As well, the British arrived in Australia in 1788 and proceeded to dispossess the Aborigines from their lands. Or we might talk about slavery, which was accepted across the globe for a long period of time. So, without delving into these issues, we can accept that attitudes in societies change, and they continue to do so.

The basic ideas still apply, and the questions remain. Are we going to look at ethics from a whole-of-society perspective, or in terms of the individual's decisions and actions? The two approaches seem to be in conflict, and neither perspective seems to be sufficient. However, are there times and places where one approach or the other might apply? Could the two approaches be made to work together? And is there something more to be said about virtue ethics?

Back to the start

When we get together and talk about ethics, we seem to think that we can work out an answer that everybody should accept. For society as a whole, the idea of the greatest good for the greatest number seems persuasive. And at an individual level, living according to moral rules, as Kant advocated, is likewise attractive. We have a responsibility to act morally. Further, keeping the question of virtue ethics in mind: what kind of person should I be? That should be enough, shouldn't it?

Then, as the sceptics have suggested, the content of virtue ethics becomes difficult, unsettled. Some modern philosophers have tried to clarify virtue ethics. Sir William David Ross (in 1930) said there are seven core values that make up a comprehensive picture of virtue:

1. Truthfulness/integrity
2. Reparation to others for wrongs
3. Gratitude
4. Justice/fairness
5. Beneficence (doing good to others, kindness)
6. Self-improvement
7. Non-maleficence (do no harm)

The difficulty is that these values cannot be made into laws. The beauty of laws is that they can define unacceptable behaviour precisely, and they can be enforced. Consider murder and stealing. Our society makes murder illegal, and it comes under Virtue 7 (non-maleficence), but we can't make non-maleficence itself into a law. Similarly with stealing. Presumably it violates Virtue 5 (beneficence), but beyond that, it is a question of how you choose to apply this virtue to yourself.

It's easy to see that there is High and Low in how a person chooses to live out these virtues, and for the most part, we could not expect the law to intrude. It can only apply in obvious, serious cases, such as assault or murder.

This seems an unsatisfactory end.

But there is a distinction here: are we discussing rules that we think should apply to all of society, or rules/principles that an individual has to decide to pursue for themselves, regardless of social norms? This raises the question: how far can we go in making and enforcing rules for everybody?

And then there is the individual question: What rules do I think I should apply to myself? This is about how we wish to live as an individual. What kind of a person do I want to be, regardless of what norms apply in my society? This could be expressed in diet; to take a simple example, people around you eat meat, but you wish to be vegetarian. You are not trying to force other people to be vegetarian; it is a rule that you wish to apply to yourself.

Ethics and society

What ethical standards should get translated into laws? This is one of the questions a discussion of ethics needs to address. The balance would seem to be between the freedom for people to pursue their own lives, and protecting the well-being of all people. This is a continuing question, as witnessed by the laws that have been proposed about hate speech in the wake of the fatal attack at Bondi Beach last December.

There are many arguments that can be made about what laws are necessary and how society and its people can be protected. And there are many arguments that are put about the nature of society, democracy, and what factors affect general behaviour. The world is clearly volatile, and different people and groups have different explanations for why it is the way it is, and what social actions would be most effective to address it.

It will not help to address these matters today.

What matters today is to distinguish between what is achievable at a political level and what we should do as individuals, for after all, regardless of what country we live in and the state of politics in that country, we are responsible for our individual actions, in our own lives and in the groups in which we are active.

First, is there a foundation value (virtue)?

We have William David Ross's list of seven values. Other writers have presented different lists.

(Note, we talk about values and virtues. It is simplest to think of values as particular qualities that people can have (brave, humble, generous etc), and of virtues as these qualities when they are held by a person.)

Here are some values that have been proposed as the foundation value:

- "Humility is the solid foundation of all virtues." — Kong Fu Zi (Confucius)
- "Courage is the ladder on which all the other virtues mount." — Clare Booth Luce (1903-1987)
- "Gratitude is not only the greatest of virtues, but the

parent of all others." — Cicero (106 BC-43 BC)

- "Self-respect is the cornerstone of all virtue." — John Herschel (1792-1871)
- "Patience is the greatest of all virtues." — Cato the Elder (234 BC-149 BC)

Only gratitude appears in William David Ross's list. Does this suggest that the whole idea of values is too vague?

The starting point is to accept that humans are complex but coherent creatures, so it would be unlikely that there was a single value that determined our ethics. At the same time, there is likely to be a package of values that paint a recognisable picture of humans.

It is best to start by going a step further back and asking: what are the things we want in life? I considered this question while exploring my family history. What was important to my forebears? Looking at all their stories, I came up with four aims in life, that seem to apply to all my ancestors:

- Competency
- Morality
- Beauty
- Love.

You can see that this is a broader canvas than ethics. But it is good to see the context that ethics fits into; ethics has to be seen in the context of all the things we find important in life. But now we see that, as people, there are lots of ways of looking at ourselves.

My suggestion is that, to look at ethics, it makes sense to do it through an understanding of what humans are in the world, physically, socially and psychologically.

A definition for ethics

But it also helps to do something we have not done yet, which is, to define ethics. Articulating a good definition helps to avoid some of the pitfalls that people encounter when they discuss ethics. The best definition I have found is that of Albert Schweitzer. He said:

"Ethics is the name we give to our concern for good behaviour. We feel an obligation to consider, not only our own personal well-being, but also that of others, society as a whole and the natural world." (1952)

He does not attempt to define "good behaviour". The assumption is that we know the difference between good behaviour and bad behaviour. We cannot pretend not to know, as some people do today. He does not demand that we ignore our own well-being; ethics does not demand that we be martyrs. However, he says that ethics inherently involves consideration of others' well-being. There are versions of ethics that claim we can serve solely our own interests and be ethical, that this is okay. But think of William David Ross's last virtue: non-maleficence.

So, I would say, doing harm to others, physically or in business, is not a "version" of ethics; it is just not ethics. (Think of Milton Friedman's definition of the goal of corporations.) This is the importance of Schweitzer's definition. Business is not exempt from ethics. And Schweitzer says we feel ethics as an obligation. We know it.

Then Schweitzer applies this definition to all the fields in which we act: with other persons, in society as a whole, and in the natural world. (Note, I added the reference to the natural world. He wrote this definition in 1952, when he was preparing a speech in acceptance of the Nobel Prize for Peace. The natural world was not yet identified as a critical area of concern. However, I think, in retrospect, he would agree with what I've done.)

Moral values

With a firm definition of ethics, we can now turn to values. I offer a set of five core human values. The beauty of this framework is that it relates to an understanding of the nature of humans. From it we can derive much longer lists of values, but it all comes from the five core values, which build up a picture of the person. I say there are five dimensions of the person.

First dimension: COGNITION. Cognition is about thinking, language, reasoning, logic, planning. Many philosophers say that morality is based on cognition. I don't think that. I think cognition is about managing ourselves and our place in the physical world, but it only does so with the cooperation of the other dimensions.

Second dimension: EMOTION. We have come to recognise that our emotions are a core part of us, and nothing happens without our emotions. This is to say that our deepest feelings and motivations drive us, even when we deny our emotions. The 'rational' decisions of managers have come to be seen as influenced by our limbic system, not merely the activity of our neocortex. This was reflected in the appearance of the concept of emotional intelligence via Daniel Goleman. So, Cognition and Emotion both contribute to our functioning.

Some of our moral decisions may elicit strong emotions, such as anxiety, love, fear and anger. However, this is not to say that emotions are equivalent to moral sensitivity. Rather, emotions may be evoked by moral sensitivity, which is the third dimension.

Third dimension: VALUING. At first, we might think that moral thinking and behaviour are the result of Cognition and Emotion working together. In fact, many people still believe that emotion is the moral part of our thinking. Many traditional philosophers had argued, conversely, that emotion was an interference in moral thinking, and should be eradicated. On the other hand, some philosophers, like David Hume, thought that morality was primarily about emotion.

However, think of Schweitzer's definition of ethics. He said we *know* what good behaviour and bad behaviour are. The quality of Valuing is seen when we apply the distinction between good and bad behaviour to our moral thinking and actions. Valuing is not something that is reducible to the emotions. It is an inner knowing. The only qualification to this is social conditioning. An example, until a few years ago, would have been a man not wearing a tie to a funeral. He would have been seen as disrespectful.

At this point we have three dimensions of the person (see Figure 3). These are the dimensions we exercise in our day-to-day functioning in the world. Each of these dimensions is associated with a moral value. Going back to Schweitzer's definition of ethics, the understanding is that humans inherently, inescapably, have a notion of good and bad behaviour. Accordingly, each of the dimensions of our functioning in the world is associated with a moral value.

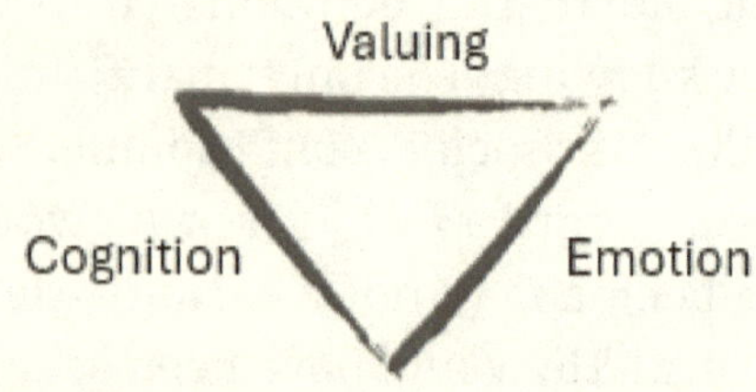

Figure 3

Core human values

Dimension 1: COGNITION. Remember, in the introduction, when I gave an exalted view of ethics, I said that the first thing we need to be is sincere and wholehearted. The value associated with Cognition is sincerity. Without sincerity, cognition is flawed and unreliable, and delivers us into falsity. When we exercise our cognition, we need to be sincere, that is, truthful with ourselves.

Thus: Cognition: Value = **Truthfulness**.

Dimension 2: EMOTION. Humans experience a wide range of emotions, from happiness to sadness, anger, fear, surprise, delight, boredom, envy and gratitude. Researchers have identified around fifty different emotions and have classified them in various ways. Any, or several, of these emotions could arise in the context of considering an ethical question. So, what would be a value that we would associate with the dimension of Emotion itself?

I say that the value is peace. Why? Because if the dimension of Emotion is to operate the way it should in our person, we need to be able to find that peaceful place in among all the emotions that could sway us and perhaps lead us astray. When we are faced with an ethical question and we are feeling, let's say, angry, fearful, ashamed, or self-righteous, the quality that will bring us to ground and allow us to make a good decision is peace.

Hence: Emotion: Value = **Peace.**

Dimension 3: VALUING. If we think about it, the dimension of Valuing is in operation most of the time. Our mind is continually perceiving our environment and also making judgements about it. To take a simple example, we buy a cup of coffee, and we smell the coffee, then we taste it. We are making use of our perception. But bundled with our perception is judgement: is the coffee hot enough, is it a nice blend of milk and water, is the coffee a pleasing taste, does it measure up to the one we had yesterday?

This is a simple example, based on perceptions. But likewise, we weigh up matters in a moral sense. Was that action (mine or another person's) right or wrong? Should I do something? What should I do? This thinking can be quite sophisticated, and the choices we envision can be quite difficult. But it is the quality of moral valuing. It is ever-present in humans.

It is present in a way that is not present in nature. When there is a very hot day or a violent thunderstorm, we don't make accusations that nature is being immoral. And we don't accuse animals of murder; we are simply more careful in the vicinity of lions. Moral Valuing is a distinctive quality of humans.

If we accept this, what value is it that is relevant to this dimension? I say it is a compound value. In Buddhism there is an eightfold path, and one of the steps is Right Action. This is usually described as consisting of fairness, justice and respect. It applies to our dealings with other people, and I would include the natural environment as part of the scope of this value.

So, Valuing: Value = Right Action (fairness, justice and respect).

These three dimensions and their corresponding values provide an adequate picture of humans as they act day-to-day. But there is more to them than this. Humans live for more than day-to-day experiences. They need to have some sense of purpose and meaning. And their lives can be animated or subdued. So, I suggest that a full picture of humans requires two more dimensions.

Dimension 4: ENERGY/SPIRIT. You know the truth of this dimension by observing a distinction, one that you can apply to yourself or to other people. Can you tell when a person is doing something with energy (or spirit) and when they are not? In the latter case, the person seems subdued, anxious, afraid or bored.

They seem to be not trying, or they are unfocused. Contrast that with a person who is "giving it their all". They are committed to what they are doing, they are enthusiastic, and they in the flow of it.

The prime example of this dimension is love and compassion. When somebody loves what they are doing, or they love a person, the love can be felt and seen. It is released and it flows into their actions. It is love that brings people to have compassion for others. We noted earlier the role of empathy, and this dimension is the full expression of it. Conversely, when someone is depressed, we say they are low in spirit.

Thus: Energy/Spirit: Value = **Love and Compassion**.

At this point we can say that this framework for ethics is inspiring. Ethics is not, as it is often perceived to be, an added burden, an additional set of rules in life we have to abide by. Ethics opens out into a space that is occupied by love, when we accept the guidance of Truthfulness, Peace and Right Action.

And there is one further dimension.

Dimension 5: IDENTITY/ PSYCHE/SOUL. At the heart of us there is.... us. We are coherent, individually definable beings. It is signified by us having our own name. I use three different labels here, because we live in changing times, and ideas are in flux. For some people, the idea of soul is unacceptable, while for others it is indispensable.

You will note that I have got this far without calling upon God, and you can see that for our purposes it is unnecessary. But I would say we are spiritual beings, despite the fact that we are surrounded by materialistic rhetoric. We live in a universe, and it has a living essence. The great signifier of this is that we recognise ethics. We recognise that there is a distinction between good and bad behaviour, as Schweitzer said.

We could call it "All-that-is", but on the understanding that there is something coherent about it. We may be uncomfortable with the word 'soul', but we can use Psyche or Identity instead. Now we might ask, what functions apply to this dimension? All the other dimensions do something.

The concern of this fifth dimension is meaning and purpose. Its core function is awareness. It is what is deepest in us. We might get from day to day without thinking about it, but in the longer term, it matters. And the quest to find a foundation for living ethically eventually opens up these deeper matters.

In this dimension, it is harder to say what the core value is, because the words seem to become interchangeable. At first, I named the core value as Insight. Later, I thought Wisdom would be appropriate. Now I think the best word is Appreciation. It expresses two aspects:

- The fifth dimension is more passive, or receptive, rather than active. It is not so much about how we act in, or upon, the world, as about how we see it. Appreciation is a receptive value rather than being action-oriented. And,
- Appreciation can be seen to grow out of the earlier dimensions, particularly the fourth: Love.

Accordingly,

Identity/Psyche/Soul: Value = **Appreciation**.

I have a diagram that presents the five core human values visually (Figure 4). It shows the first three dimensions (and values) as a triangle, to mean that the three aspects of Cognition, Emotion and Valuing are each necessary, and as three lines together, they are complete. The unit is stable, strong and functional. On top of the triangle there are two extra lines, for energy/spirit and soul/ psyche/ identity. This is to say that for the person to fulfil their complete human potential, they need these two dimensions as well, even though they may not be apparent at first glance.

In addition, unless the three dimensions of the triangle are operating with good health, these top two dimensions will atrophy and fade into the background. The five lines together paint a dynamic picture of a human in the world.

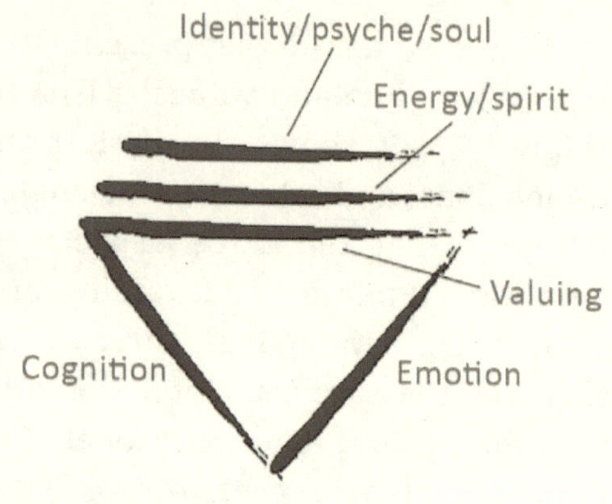

Figure 4

Where is the world?

This question is to remind us that we live in a body, and we live in a social and material reality called the world. What can be said about that?

Figure 5 seeks to show the relationships. The image depicts a person in their environment. We are inseparable from our bodies and our environment, just as our cognitive activity is not separated from our emotions. Note there are four aspects of this world. Two aspects are about our connection to our physical body and our material, physical world. The other two aspects are social: our interpersonal relationships and our broader social context.

You could say that for each aspect there is something *near* (our body or our interpersonal environment) and something *far*: the broader physical world - home, neighbourhood, far-off places; and the broader social environment - towns, states, nations.

Given the principles stated here, these different environments can be explored. We can examine each of the core values and see how they apply in each of these areas. That is for another day.

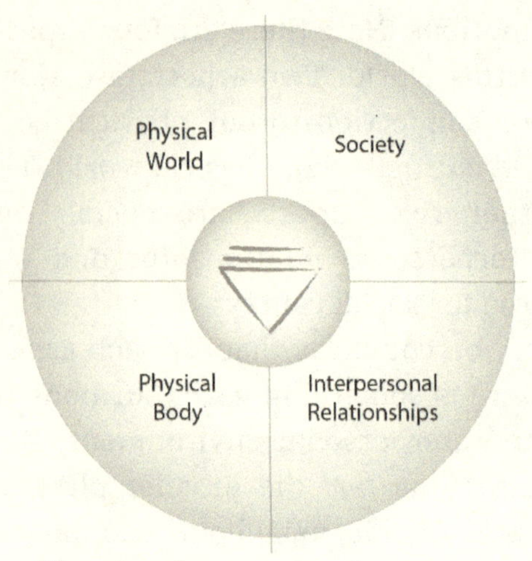

Figure 5

Are there other values?

As with the emotions, there are many further values. Some different systems have 24, 64, or 124 values in all. It doesn't matter. We are dealing with language, and the sometimes subtle differences between words. I have constructed tables with lists of values grouped according to the five core values. This seems to make sense, but it can also lead to arguments about which core value that a particular value belongs with. They are not important arguments, but they may provide some new insights.

Do people evolve or develop in ethics?

it is useful to describe a spectrum of ethical behaviour, because it would be naïve to think everyone has the same understanding about ethics or the same level of commitment to it. And we know there are people who express the right rhetoric about doing good, but their behaviour tells you a different story. They have all the right words, but their only intent is to put you off the scent. Other people have a high commitment to living ethically, even going beyond that and living a life of noble service to others and society.

We can talk about seven types of orientation towards ethics. The first type, or level, is the person who resists any constraints upon their actions. Their interest is self-interest; they have no concern for anyone else. Nor do they have any respect for the law. They will do whatever they can get away with. They might pay lip service to the law, but only because that serves their purposes.

The second level is people who obey the law, even if grudgingly, but they don't do more than the law requires. In the business world, these are the companies that do immoral things but defend their actions by saying they were acting in accordance with the law. By saying they do immoral things, I mean they do things that we would all accept were immoral. They tend to see it quite literally though, and will justify actions on the grounds that they are legal, even if they are morally poor or questionable.

At the third level, the emphasis shifts, and relationships come into the foreground. The idea of loyalty emerges. However, there are boundaries around loyalty. One has loyalty to one's own people - the people in my family, my close friends or my group or organisation. There is no sense of loyalty or obligation towards people who are outside of these boundaries. This is the idea of belonging, the idea that you belong to some group, and you look after each other. (This suggests Maslow's hierarchy of needs.)

The fourth level shows another shift. The focus is still on relationships, but the focus is broader. The values of fairness, justice and respect come to the fore. It is broader because the person recognises that their obligation to act ethically extends beyond their own group, beyond one's own family, friends or organisation.

The fifth level deepens the emphasis on relationships. Here, ethics is seen as building high-quality relationships, so being trustworthy and establishing trust in relationships comes to the fore. Ethics are accepted now as a set of human values that apply across communities. The person's focus is on right conduct towards all others, including people who would have been seen formerly as outsiders.

You could say that ethics doesn't really appear until the third or fourth level. What is emerging in conjunction with it is empathy. Beginning at the third level, people start to consider how another person feels. This is why they begin to act in consideration of other people's well-being. From here on, as a person develops from one level to another, empathy becomes more important.

The sixth level is about the person taking positive action in communities and society to foster higher human values. It's about fostering positive change. It is about more than just adherence to moral rules. This level describes people who seek to enhance the well-being of society.

The seventh level is about a personal vision of ethics (and of life) that seeks to bring the whole of earth and its people into harmony, and to fulfil its potential. That sounds grand, but that's how it should end up. The person's focus is on social responsibility, service, sustainability and future generations.

What happens when you consider yourself in relation to these levels? Do people fit into one of these boxes? We could say that a given level is more characteristic of a person than the others, but that could change over time or in different contexts. This is to say, a person may develop over time.

Here is a summary of the seven levels of ethics.

Level 1: Opposed to any restraint on their conduct, including the law; self-interest rules.

Level 2: Accept compliance with the law, but go no further morally.

Level 3: Support members of their own family, group, organisation; loyal to them.

Level 4: Exercise values of fairness, justice and respect towards other people generally.

Level 5: Show trustworthiness and build high-quality relationships with others.

Level 6: Exercise initiative in communities to enhance higher human values.

Level 7: Exhibit a personal vision for the well-being of all people and the planet.

How does development occur?

The idea of seven levels of ethics suggests that people can develop in ethics. We learn through experiences, good and bad, through reflection, encountering wise and inspiring people, reading good books, having role models, and supportive friends.

Having different levels of ethics explains why many conversations about ethics are confused and unproductive. People are coming at it from different levels, and they are trying to defend their own stance. This is made more difficult because, in the public arena, people tend to talk at around Levels 4 and 5. So, publicly, everyone talks as if we all agreed that we should be truthful, fair, just and respectful towards others.

The next issue to examine is why people act the way they do, and why they justify their conduct. Each level of ethics is driven by a given perception of the world, a worldview. The person who is unethical and who pursues only their own interests is driven by a view of the world where they think they need to look after themselves, and grasp what they can, or they will not survive. They think that dominating others is the only way to ensure this.

Figure 6 collapses the seven levels down into three. The first level, about law, includes two sorts of people. One type tries to get away with as much as they can. The other type obeys the law, but only literally. They are not interested in the spirit of the law.

The second level here compresses three of the levels we just described. It is about relationships. At first, people support members of their own group, but their commitment extends no further. This evolves into accepting that fairness, justice and respect must be applied generally, to all people, not just the people in our own group. And this evolves into building high-quality relationships with other people, based on trust and caring.

The last level is about Identity, and there are two levels here. The first level is about working in communities to enhance human well-being, and lastly, it is about extending this vision to the whole planet.

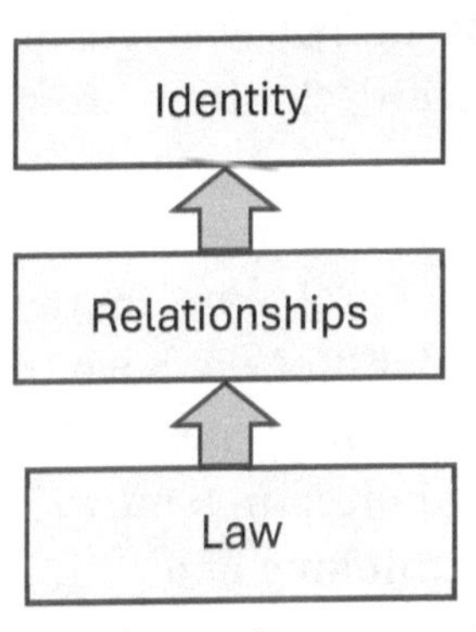

"I am committed to living out high human values."

"I act respectfully and caringly towards others."

"I comply with laws and rules."

Figure 6

How do you apply this knowledge in your own life?

The first step in applying this in your own life is to go back to the definition of ethics as Albert Schweitzer articulated it. The essence of ethics is to be fair to other people, and to do no harm. The problem is that we are asked to do that in the world as it is. Often it will be difficult. You can think of the classic scenario of the mother or father who steals bread to stop their children from starving to death.

One thing to remember is that it's one thing to solve problems in the abstract, but in "real life" we have to make decisions in particular circumstances, and often in a hurry.

Central to our thinking and acting is our motivations. It is good to think of people at the different levels of ethics and ask, what is the person's motivation? And why do they think that way? How do they see the world? Can we live differently to that? Can we live up to a higher ideal? These are deep questions. Absorbing yourself in them will open up a host of other questions, just as the five core human values open out into a host of other values, as shown in Figure 7.

Cognition → Truth
Honesty, Integrity, Sincerity, Trustworthiness, Competence, Curiosity, Reliability
Emotion → Peace
Peacefulness, Calmness, Harmony, Cheerfulness, Patience, Self-discipline, Moderation
Valuing → Right Action
Responsibility, Respect, Fairness, Justice, Dignity, Courage, Honour, Loyalty, Duty, Selflessness
Energy/Spirit → Love
Compassion, Enthusiasm, Sense of community, Friendliness, Grace, Joy, Benevolence, Kindness, Creativity

Soul/Identity/Psyche → Appreciation
Awareness, Consciousness, Purpose, Meaning, Forgiveness, Wisdom, Contentment, Reverence, Humility, Wonder

Figure 7

Note, at particular times in our life, one or another value might come to the fore. Example (from family history): Gordon Fink, who died at Gallipoli, needed to prove that he could be brave. Had he lived, other values would have come to the fore.

The five core values can be expressed as principles for living:

1. Be truthful.
2. Be a maker of peace.
3. Right action: be fair, just, respectful.
4. Be compassionate and kind.
5. Appreciate all that is given.

We can expand this into the following admonitions to ourselves.

I recognise that I am present in this world as an individual in the midst of others, and I carry responsibility for my thoughts, words and actions. Accordingly:

I will be honest in my thinking and in what I say, and I will act with integrity, honouring the truth and not seeking to deceive.

I will be conscious of my feelings and the feelings of others, remembering that peacefulness is the foundation for constructive action.

I will observe the principles of Right Action, seeking to be ethical and unselfish; I will be fair, respectful and just, contributing to the well-being of others and the natural world.

I will allow the spirit and energy of love, compassion and kindness to infuse my actions, and to flow out towards others.

I will remember that consciousness is the first gift of the universe, and contained within it is meaning, purpose and bliss, in every moment, and I will respond to the universe with appreciation.

Always remember that your true nature is virtuous. By diligently practising the virtues of life, you will reach purity and clarity of being."

Hua-Ching Ni (2007, p. 244)

Other books by Glenn Martin

Stories/Reflections on experience

The Ten Thousand Things (2010)
Sustenance (2011)
To the Bush and Back to Business (2012)
The Big Story Falls Apart (2014)
The Quilt Approach: A Tasmanian Patchwork (2020)
Long Time Approaching: An Incomplete Memoir (2023)
Travel with a Pen (2023)
Library Meets Book Fair (2024)
The Traveller, Lost (2026)

Books on family history

A Modest Quest (2017)
The Search for Edward Lewis (2018)
They Went to Australia (2019)
No Gold in Melbourne: A Scottish Family in Australia (2021)
All the Rivers Come Together: Tracing Family (2022)

The Sailor, the Baron and the Dressmaker (2024)
Ordinary People, Remarkable Lives (2025)

Poetry collections
Flames in the Open (2007)
Love and Armour (2007)
Volume 4: I in the Stream (2017)
Volume 3: That Was Then: The Early Poems Project (2019)
The Way Is Open (2020)

Local history
Places in the Bush: A History of Kyogle Shire (1988)
The Kyogle Public School Centenary Book (1995)

www.ingramcontent.com/pod-product-compliance
Lightning Source LLC
LaVergne TN
LVHW050945080826
845145LV00004B/1421

* 9 7 8 1 7 6 4 4 1 1 4 1 7 *